THE DISCOVERY OF GLACIER BAY (1879)
by John Muir

DRAWN BY J. A. FRASER, FROM A SKETCH MADE BY THE AUTHOR IN 1879. ENGRAVED BY CHARLES STATE.
THE PACIFIC GLACIER.
View of the front of Pacific Glacier from the head of Pacific Fiord, head of Glacier Bay.

EDITOR'S PREFACE

Who better to discover Alaska's Glacier Bay than John Muir? He had advanced the glacier theory for California's Yosemite Valley—in spite of heavy opposition from the leading expert—and then extended the idea up the West Coast clear to Alaska. To be sure, Muir did not develop the theory that ice could erode mountain valleys. That had been done by Louis Agassiz. Muir's contribution was to lie on the rocks, as the glaciers had done, he said, and with "patient brooding" to inquire whither the ice had come and whence it went. In the process he discovered yosemite valleys by the score (using the lower case y to differentiate the general use of this term) and even coined the adjective yosemitic.

In Alaska he earned the name "Ice Chief" and spent several "icy summers" exploring and learning. It was in 1879, late in the year, when he pushed his luck to the limit and explored Glacier Bay. Some years afterward, in 1895, *Century Magazine* (a national periodical of that early day) published his account of that discovery. It is from this article that the present booklet is reprinted. Illustrations also come from that same source, with a few others added from an 1897 *Century*.

All John Muir buffs, Alaska fans, Glacier Bay visitors, and even Yosemite visitors will find interest and excitement in Muir's account. Later, Muir's 1901 book, *Our National Parks*, described several existing and proposed park areas with a plea for their conservation. It apparently had some effect, although belated and indirect, for Glacier Bay National Monument was proclaimed in 1925, and is today the largest area in America's entire National Park System. Here is the monument's beginning.

William R. Jones   former Chief Park Naturalist
Yosemite National Park

Copyright © 1981 OUTBOOKS, 217 Kimball Avenue, Golden, Colorado 80401
ISBN 0-89646-045-2

VIEW OF PART OF MUIR GLACIER, LOOKING NORTHWEST FROM TREE MOUNTAIN, SHOWING MEDIAL MORAINES.

THE DISCOVERY OF GLACIER BAY.
BY ITS DISCOVERER.
John Muir.

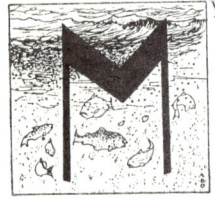

My first visit to the now famous Glacier Bay of Alaska was made toward the end of October, 1879, when young ice was beginning to form in the branch inlets occupied by the glaciers, and the mountains were mantled with fresh snow all the way down from the highest peaks and ridges of the Fairweather Range nearly to the level of the sea.

I had spent most of the season exploring the cañon of the Stickeen River and its glaciers, and a small portion of the interior region beyond the Coast Mountains, on the divide of some of the southerly tributaries of the Yukon and Mackenzie rivers. When I got back to my headquarters at Fort Wrangel, about the beginning of October, it seemed too late for new undertakings in this icy northland. The days were growing short, and winter, with its heavy storms, was drawing nigh, when avalanches would be booming down the long white slopes of the peaks, and all the land would be buried. But, on the other hand, though this white wilderness was new to me, I was familiar with storms, and enjoyed them, knowing well that in right relations with them they are ever kindly. The main inland channels, extending in every direction along the coast, remain open all winter; and their shores being well forested, it would be easy to keep warm in camp, while in a large canoe abundance of provisions could be carried. I determined, therefore, to go ahead as far north as possible, with or without companions, to see and learn what I could, especially with reference to future work. When I made known my plans to Mr. Young, the Wrangel missionary, he offered to go with me, and with his assistance I procured a good canoe and a crew of Indians, gathered a large stock of provisions, blankets, etc., and on October 14 set forth, eager to welcome whatever wildness might offer, so long as food and firewood should last.

Our crew numbered four: Toyatte, a grand old Stickeen nobleman, who was elected captain, not only because he owned the canoe, but for his skill in woodcraft and seamanship; Kadechan, the son of a Chilcat chief; John, a Stickeen who acted as interpreter; and Sitka Charlie. Mr. Young is one of those fearless and adventurous evangelists who in seeking to save others save themselves, and it was the opportunities the trip might afford to meet the Indians of the different tribes along our route that induced him to join me.

After all our bundles were stowed aboard, and we were about to cast loose from the wharf, Kadechan's mother, a woman of great natural dignity and force of character, came down the steps alongside the canoe, oppressed with anxious fears for the safety of her son. Standing silent for a few moments, she held the missionary with her dark, bodeful eyes, and at length, with great solemnity of speech and gesture, accused him of using undue influence in gaining her son's consent to go on a dangerous voyage among tribes that were unfriendly to the Stickeens. Then, like an ancient sibyl, she foretold a long train of disasters from stormwinds and ice, and in awful majesty of mother-love finished by saying: "If my son comes not back, on you will be his blood, and you shall pay. I say it." Mr. Young tried in vain to calm her fears, promising Heaven's care as well as his own for her precious son, assuring her that he would faithfully share every danger that might assail him, and, if need be, willingly die in his defense. "We shall see whether or not you die," she said as she turned away.

Toyatte also encountered domestic difficulties in getting away. When he stepped into the canoe I noticed a cloud on his grand old face, as if his sad doom, now drawing near, was already beginning to overshadow him. When he took leave of his wife she wept bitterly, saying that the Chilcat chiefs would surely kill him in case he should escape the winter storms. But it was not on this trip that the old hero was to meet his fate, and when we were fairly free in the wilderness these gloomy forebodings vanished, and a gentle breeze pressed us joyfully onward over the shining waters.

We first pursued a westerly course through Sumner Strait, between Kupreanof and Prince of Wales islands; then, turning northward, we sailed up the charming Kiku Strait, through the midst of innumerable picturesque islets, across Prince Frederick Sound, up Chatham Strait, and thence northwestward through Icy Strait and around Glacier Bay. Thence, returning through Icy Strait, we urged our way up the grand Lynn Canal to the Davidson Glacier and Chilcat, and returned to Wrangel along the coast of the mainland, visiting the icy Sum Dum Bay and the Le Conte Glacier on our route. Thus we made a journey more than eight hundred miles long; and though hardships were encountered, and a few dangers, the wild wonderland made compensation beyond our most extravagant hopes.

The first stages of our journey were mostly enjoyment. The weather was about half bright, and we glided along the green and yellow shores in comfort, the lovely islands passing in harmonious succession, like ideas in a fine poem. The rain did not hinder us, but when the wind was too wild we stayed in camp, the Indians usually improving such storm times in deer-hunting, while I examined the rocks and woods. Most of our camps were made in nooks that were charmingly embowered, and fringed with bushes and late flowers. After supper we sat long around the fire, listening to the stories of the Indians about the wild animals they were acquainted with, their hunting adventures, wars, traditions, religion, and customs. Every Indian party we met we interviewed, and every village we came to we visited. Thus passed our days and nights until we reached the west coast of Admiralty Island, intending to make a straight course thence up Lynn Canal, when we learned from a party of traveling Hoonas that the Chilcats had been drinking and quarreling, that Kadechan's father had been shot, and that we could not go safely into their country before these whisky quarrels were settled. My Indians evidently believed this news, and dreaded the consequences; therefore I decided to turn to the westward through Icy Strait, and to go in search of the wonderful ice-mountains to which Sitka Charlie, the youngest of my crew, had frequently referred. Having noticed my interest in glaciers, he told me that when he was a boy he had gone with his father to hunt seals in a large bay full of ice, and that he thought he could find it if I cared to have him try. I was rejoiced to find all the crew now willing to go on this adventure, judging, perhaps, that ice-mountains under the present circumstances might prove less dangerous than Chilcats.

On the 24th, about noon, as we came near a small island in Icy Strait, Charlie said that we must procure some dry wood there, for in the ice-mountain country which we were now approaching not a single tree of any kind could be found. This seemed strange news to the rest of the crew, and I had to make haste to end an angry dispute that was rising by ordering as much wood to be taken aboard as we could carry. Then we set sail direct for the ice-country, holding a northwesterly course until long after dark, when we reached a small inlet that sets in near the mouth of Glacier Bay, on the west side. Here we made a cold camp on a desolate snow-covered beach in stormy sleet and darkness. At daybreak I looked eagerly in every direction to learn what kind of place we were in; but gloomy rain-clouds covered the mountains, and I could see nothing that could give me a clue, while Vancouver's chart, hitherto a faithful guide, here failed us altogether. Nevertheless, we made haste to be off; and fortunately, just as we were leaving the shore, a faint smoke was seen across the inlet, toward which Charlie, who now seemed lost, gladly steered. Our sudden appearance so early that gray morning had evidently alarmed our neighbors, for as soon as we were within hailing distance an Indian with his face blackened fired a shot over our heads, and in a blunt, bellowing voice roared, "Who are you?" Our interpreter shouted, "Friends and the Fort Wrangel missionary." Then men, women, and children swarmed out of the hut, and awaited our approach on the beach. One of the hunters having brought his gun with him, Kadechan sternly rebuked him, asking with superb indignation whether he was not ashamed to bring a gun in his hand to meet a missionary. Friendly relations, however, were speedily established, and as a cold rain was falling, they invited us into their hut. It seemed small for two persons; nevertheless, twenty-one managed to find shelter in it about a smoky fire. Our hosts proved to be Hoona seal-hunters laying in their winter stores of meat and skins. The packed hut was passably well ventilated, but its oily, meaty smells were not the same to our noses as those of the briny, sprucy nooks we were accustomed to, and the circle of black eyes peering at us through a fog of reek and smoke made a novel picture. We were glad, however, to get within reach of information, and of course asked many questions concerning the ice-mountains and the strange bay, to most of which our inquisitive Hoona friends replied with counter-questions as to our object in coming to such a place, especially so late in the year. They had heard of Mr. Young and his work at Fort Wrangel, but could not understand what a missionary could be doing in such a place as this. Was he going to preach to seals and gulls, they asked, or to the ice-mountains? and could they take his word? Then John explained that only the friend of the missionary was seeking ice-mountains; that Mr. Young had already preached many good words in the villages we had visited on our way, in their own among the rest; that our hearts were good; and that every Indian was our friend. Then we gave them a little rice, sugar, tea, and tobacco, after which they began to gain confidence and to speak freely. They told us that the main bay was called by them Sit-a-da-kay, or Ice Bay; that there were many large ice-mountains in it, but no gold-

Mount Reid.

ENGRAVED BY C. SCHWARZBURGER.

A MORAINE—STREAKED PORTION OF MUIR GLACIER ON THE EAST SIDE, LOOKING TOWARD HOWLING VALLEY.

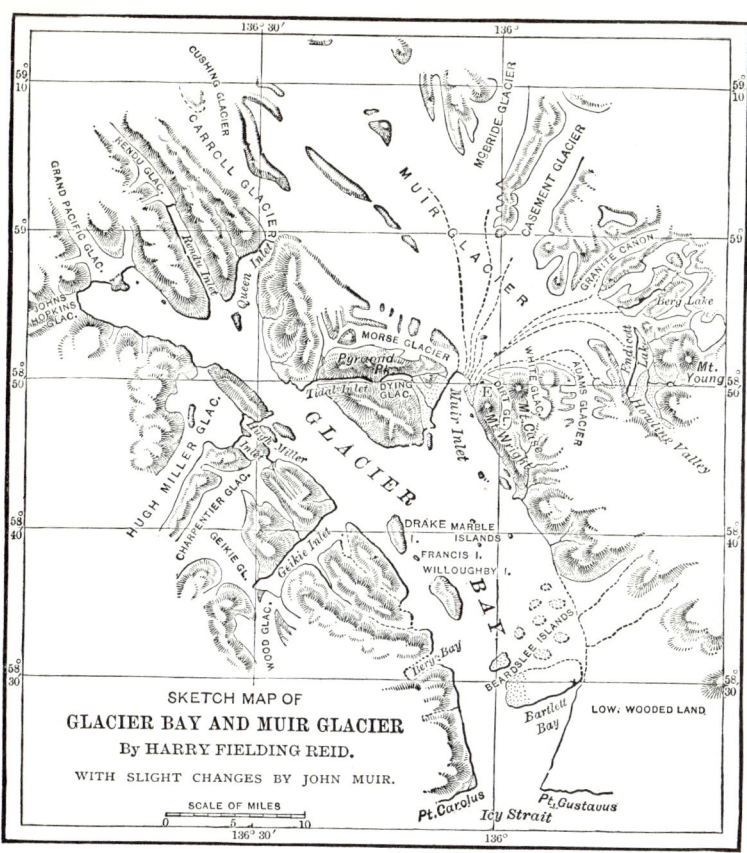

SKETCH MAP OF GLACIER BAY AND MUIR GLACIER
By HARRY FIELDING REID.
WITH SLIGHT CHANGES BY JOHN MUIR.

mines; and that the ice-mountain they knew best was at the head of the bay, where most of the seals were found.

Notwithstanding the rain, I was anxious that we should push and grope our way beneath the clouds as best we could, in case worse weather should come; but Charlie was ill at ease, and wanted one of the seal-hunters to go with us, for the place was much changed. I promised to pay well for a guide, and in order to lighten the canoe proposed to leave most of our heavy stores with our friends until our return. After a long consultation one of them consented to go. His wife got ready his blanket and a piece of cedar matting for his bed, and some provisions — mostly dried salmon, and seal sausage made of strips of lean meat plaited around a core of fat. She followed us to the beach, and just as we were pushing off said with a pretty smile: "It is my husband that you are taking away. See that you bring him back." We got under way about 10 A. M. The wind was in our favor, but a cold rain pelted us, and we could see but little of the dreary, treeless wilderness which we had now fairly entered. The bitter blast, however, gave us good speed; our bedraggled canoe rose and fell on the icy waves, solemnly bowing to them, and mimicking the gestures of a big ship. Our course was northwestward, up the southwest side of the bay, near the shore of what seemed to be the mainland, some smooth marble islands being on our right. About noon we discovered the first of the great glaciers — the one I afterward named for Geikie, the noted Scotch geologist. Its lofty blue cliffs, looming up through the draggled skirts of the clouds, gave a tremendous impression of savage power, while the roar of the new-born icebergs thickened and emphasized the general roar of the storm. An hour and a half beyond the Geikie Glacier we ran into a slight harbor where the shore is low, dragged the canoe beyond the reach of drifting icebergs, and, much against my desire to push ahead, encamped, the guide insisting that the big ice-mountain at the head of the bay could not be reached before dark, that the landing there was dangerous even in daylight, and that this was the only safe harbor on the way to it. While camp was being made I strolled along the shore to examine the rocks and the fossil timber that abound here. All the rocks are freshly glaciated even below the sea-level, nor have the waves as yet worn off the surface polish, much less the heavy scratches and grooves and lines of glacial contour.

The next day being Sunday, the minister wished to stay in camp; and so, on account of the weather, did the Indians. I therefore set out on an excursion, and spent the day alone on the mountain slopes above the camp, and to the north of it, to see what I might learn. Pushing on through rain and mud and sludgy snow, crossing many brown, boulder-choked torrents, wading, jumping, wallowing in snow to my shoulders, I had a desperately hard and dangerous time. After crouching cramped and benumbed in the canoe, poulticed in wet clothes and blankets night and day, my limbs had been long asleep. This day they were awake, and in the hour of trial proved that they had not lost the cunning learned on many a mountain peak of the high Sierra. I reached a height of 1500 feet, on the ridge that bounds the second of the great glaciers on the south. All the landscape was smothered in clouds, and I began to fear that I had climbed in vain, as far as wide views were concerned. But at length the clouds lifted a little, and beneath their gray fringes I saw the berg-filled expanse of the bay, and the feet of the mountains that stand about it, and the imposing fronts of five of the huge glaciers, the nearest being immediately beneath me. This was my first general view of Glacier Bay, a solitude of ice and snow and new-born rocks, dim, dreary, mysterious. I held the ground I had so dearly won for an hour or two, sheltering myself as best I could from the blast, while with benumbed fingers I sketched what I could see of the landscape, and wrote a few lines in my note-book. Then I breasted the snow again, crossed the muffled, shifting avalanche tali, forded the torrents in safety, and reached camp about dark, wet and weary, but rich in a notable experience.

While I was getting some coffee, Mr. Young told me that the Indians were discouraged, and had been talking about turning back, fearing that I would be lost, or that in some way the expedition would come to grief if I persisted in going farther. They had been asking him what possible motive I could have in climbing dangerous mountains when blinding storms were blowing; and when he replied that I was only seeking knowledge, Toyatte said, " Muir must be a witch to seek knowledge in such a place as this, and in such miserable weather." After supper, crouching about a dull fire of fossil wood, they became still more doleful, and talked in tones that accorded well with the growling torrents about us, and with the wind and rain among the rocks, telling sad old stories of crushed canoes and drowned Indians, and of hunters lost and frozen in snow-storms.

Toyatte, dreading the treeless, forlorn appearance of the region, said that his heart was not strong, and that he feared his canoe, on the safety of which our lives depended, might be entering a skookum-house (jail) of ice, from which there might be no escape; while the Hoona guide said bluntly that if I was so fond of danger, and meant to go close up to the noses of the ice-mountains, he would not consent to go any farther: for we should all be lost, as many of his tribe had been, by the sudden rising of bergs from the bottom. They seemed to be losing heart with every howl of the storm, and fearing that they might fail me now that I was in the midst of so grand a congregation of glaciers, which possibly I might not see again, I made haste to reassure them, telling them that for ten years I had wandered alone among mountains and storms, and that good luck always followed me; that with me, therefore, they need fear nothing; that the storm would soon cease, and the sun would shine; and that Heaven cared for us, and guided us all the time, whether we knew it or not: but that only brave men had a right to look for Heaven's care, therefore all childish fear must be put away. This little speech did good. Kadechan, with some show of enthusiasm, said he liked to travel with good-luck people; and dignified old Toyatte declared that now his heart was strong again, and he would venture on with me as far as I liked, for my "wawa" was "delait" (my talk was very good). The old warrior even became a little sentimental, and said that if the canoe were crushed he would not greatly care, because on the way to the other world he would have pleasant companions.

Next morning it was still raining and snowing, but the wind was from the south, and swept us bravely forward, while the bergs were cleared from our course. In about an hour we reached the second of the big glaciers, which I afterward named for Hugh Miller. We rowed up its fiord, and landed to make a slight examination of its grand frontal wall. The berg-producing portion we found to be about a mile and a half wide. It presents an imposing array of jagged spires and pyramids, and flat-topped towers and battlements, of many shades of blue, from pale, shimmering, limpid tones in the crevasses and hollows, to the most startling, chilling, almost shrieking vitriol blue on the plain mural spaces from which bergs had just been discharged. Back from the front for a few miles the surface is rendered inaccessible by a series of wide, weathered crevasses, with the spaces between them rising like steps, as if the entire mass of this portion of the glacier had sunk in successive sections as it reached deep water, and the sea had found its way beneath it. Beyond this

GENERAL VIEW OF MUIR GLACIER, FROM THE EAST SIDE NEAR THE FRONT, LOOKING NORTH.

the glacier extends indefinitely in a gently rising prairie-like expanse, and branches among the slopes and cañons of the Fairweather Range.

From here a run of two hours brought us to the head of the bay, and to the mouth of the northwest fiord, at the head of which lie the Hoona sealing-grounds, and the great glacier now called the Pacific, and another called the Hoona. The fiord is about five miles long, and is two miles wide at the mouth. Here the Hoona guide had a store of dry wood, which we took aboard. Then, setting sail, we were driven wildly up the fiord, as if the storm-wind were saying: "Go, then, if you will, into my icy chamber; but you shall stay until I am ready to let you out." All this time sleety rain was falling on the bay, and snow on the mountains; but soon after we landed the sky began to open. The camp was made on a rocky bench near the front of the Pacific Glacier, and the canoe was carried beyond reach of the bergs and berg-waves. The bergs were now crowded in a dense pack against the ice-wall, as if the storm-wind had determined to make the glacier take back her crystal offspring and keep them at home.

While camp affairs were being attended to, I set out to climb a mountain for comprehensive views; and before I had reached a height of a thousand feet the rain ceased, and the clouds began to rise from the lower altitudes, slowly lifting their white skirts, and lingering in majestic, wing-shaped masses about the mountains that rise out of the broad, icy sea. These were the highest and whitest of all the white mountains, and the greatest of all the glaciers I had yet seen. Climbing higher for a still broader outlook, I made notes and sketched, improving the precious time while sunshine streamed through the luminous fringes of the clouds, and fell on the green waters of the fiord, the glittering bergs, the crystal bluffs of the two vast glaciers, the intensely white, far-spreading fields of ice, and the ineffably chaste and spiritual heights of the Fairweather Range, which were now hidden, now partly revealed, the whole making a picture of icy wildness unspeakably pure and sublime.

Looking southward, a broad ice-sheet was seen extending in a gently undulating plain from the Pacific Fiord in the foreground to the horizon, dotted and ridged here and there with mountains which were as white as the snow-covered ice in which they were half, or more than half, submerged. Several of the great glaciers flow from this one grand fountain. It is an instructive example of a general glacier covering the hills and dales of a country that is not yet ready to be brought to the light of

DRAWN BY J. A. FRASER, FROM A PHOTOGRAPH BY REID. FRONT OF MUIR GLACIER, FROM MOUNT WRIGHT. ENGRAVED BY C. SCHWARZBURGER.

DRAWN BY J. A. FRASER, FROM A PHOTOGRAPH. ENGRAVED BY ROBERT VARLEY.

VIEW OF FOSSIL FOREST NEAR THE FRONT OF MUIR GLACIER, ON THE WEST SIDE.

day — not only covering, but creating, a landscape with all the features it is destined to have when, in the fullness of time, the fashioning ice-sheet shall be lifted by the sun, and the land shall become warm and fruitful. The view to the westward is bounded and almost filled by the glorious Fairweather Mountains, the highest of them springing aloft in sublime beauty to a height of nearly 16,000 feet, while from base to summit every peak and spire and dividing ridge of all the mighty host was of a spotless, solid white, as if painted. It would seem that snow could never be made to lie on the steepest slopes and precipices unless plastered on when wet, and then frozen. But this snow could not have been wet. It must have been fixed by being driven and set in small particles like the storm-dust of drifts, which, when in this condition, is fixed not only on sheer cliffs, but in massive overcurling cornices. Along the base of this majestic range sweeps the Pacific Glacier, fed by innumerable cascading tributaries, and discharging into the head of the fiord by two mouths, each nearly a mile wide. This is the largest of all the Glacier Bay glaciers that are at all river-like, the trunk of the larger Muir Glacier being more like a lake than a river. After the continuous rainy or snowy weather which we had had since leaving Wrangel, the clear weather was most welcome. Dancing down the mountain to camp, my mind glowing like the sun-beaten glaciers, I found the Indians seated around a good fire, entirely happy now that the farthest point of the journey had been reached. How keenly bright were the stars that night in the frosty sky, and how impressive was the thunder of the icebergs, rolling, swelling, reverberating through the solemn stillness! I was too happy to sleep.

About daylight next morning we crossed the fiord, and landed on the south side of the island that divides the front wall of the Pacific Glacier. The whiskered faces of seals dotted the water between the bergs, and I could not prevent John and Charlie and Kadechan from shooting at them. Fortunately, they were not skilled in this kind of hunting, and few, if any, were hurt. Leaving the Indians in charge of the canoe, I climbed the island, and gained a good general view of the glacier. At one favorable place I descended about fifty feet below the side of the glacier, where its denuding, fashioning action was clearly shown. Pushing back from here, I found the surface crevassed and sunken in steps, like the Hugh Miller Glacier, as if it were being undermined by the action of the tide-waters. For a distance of fifteen or twenty miles the river-like ice-flood is nearly level, and when it recedes the ocean water will follow it, and thus form a long extension of the fiord, with features essentially the same as those

Mount Lituya.   Mount Fairweather.

DRAWN BY J. A. FRASER, FROM A SKETCH MADE BY THE AUTHOR IN 1890.   ENGRAVED BY R. C. COLLINS.

FAIRWEATHER RANGE, FROM GLACIER BAY.

now extending into the continent farther south, where many great glaciers once poured into the sea, though scarce a vestige of them now exists. Thus the domain of the sea has been, and is being, extended in these ice-sculptured lands, and the scenery of the shores is enriched. The dividing island is about a thousand feet high, and is hard beset by the glacier, which still crushes heavily against and around it. A short time ago its summit was at least two thousand feet below the surface of the over-sweeping ice; now three hundred feet of the top is free, and under present climatic conditions it will soon be wholly free from the ice, and will take its place as a glacier-polished island in the middle of the fiord, like a thousand others in this magnificent archipelago. Emerging from its icy sepulcher, it gives a most telling illustration of the birth of a marked feature of a landscape. In this instance it is not the mountain, but the glacier, that is in labor, and the mountain itself is being brought forth.

The Hoona Glacier enters the fiord on the south side, a short distance below the Pacific, displaying a broad and far-reaching expanse, over which many of the lofty peaks of the Fairweather Range are seen; but the front wall, thrust into the fiord, is not nearly so interesting as that of the Pacific, and I did not observe any bergs discharged from it.

After we had seen the unveiling of the majestic peaks and glaciers that evening, and their baptism in the down-pouring sunbeams, it was inconceivable that nature could have anything finer to show us. Nevertheless, compared with what was coming the next morning, all that was as nothing. As far as we could see, the lovely dawn gave no promise of anything uncommon. Its most impressive features were the frosty clearness of the sky, and a deep, brooding calm, made all the more striking by the intermittent thunder of the bergs. The sunrise we did not see at all, for we were beneath the shadows of the fiord cliffs; but in the midst of our studies we were startled by the sudden appearance of a red light burning with a strange, unearthly splendor on the topmost peak of the Fairweather Mountains. Instead of vanishing as suddenly as it had appeared, it spread and spread until the whole range down to the level of the glaciers was filled with the celestial fire. In color it was at first a vivid crimson, with a thick, furred appearance, as fine as the alpenglow, yet indescribably rich and deep — not in the least like a garment or mere external flush or bloom through which one might expect to see the rocks or snow, but every mountain apparently glowing from the heart like molten metal fresh from a furnace. Beneath the frosty shadows of the fiord we stood hushed and awe-stricken, gazing at the holy vision; and had we seen the heavens open and God made manifest, our attention could not have been more tremendously strained. When the highest peak began to burn, it did not seem to be steeped in sunshine, however glorious, but rather as if it had been thrust into the body of the sun itself. Then the supernal fire slowly descending, with a sharp line of demarkation separating it from the cold, shaded region beneath, peak after peak, with their spires and ridges and cascading glaciers, caught the heavenly glow, until all the mighty host stood transfigured, hushed, and thoughtful, as if awaiting the coming of the Lord. The white, rayless light of the morning, seen when I was alone amid the silent peaks of the Sierra, had always seemed to me the most telling of the terrestrial manifestations of God. But here the mountains themselves were made divine, and declared his glory in terms still more impressive. How long we gazed I never knew. The glorious vision passed away in a gradual, fading change through a thousand tones of color to pale yellow and white, and then the work of the ice-world went on again in every-day beauty. The green waters of the fiord were filled with sun-spangles; with the upspringing breeze the fleet of icebergs set forth on their voyages; and on the innumerable mirrors and prisms of these bergs, and on those of the shattered crystal walls of the glaciers, common white light and rainbow light began to glow, while the mountains, changing to stone, put on their frosty jewelry, and loomed again in the thin azure in serene terrestrial majesty. We turned and sailed away, joining the outgoing bergs, while "Gloria in excelsis" still seemed to be sounding over all the white landscape, and our burning hearts were ready for any fate, feeling that whatever the future might have in store, the treasures we had gained would enrich our lives forever.

When we arrived at the mouth of the fiord, and rounded the massive granite headland that stands guard at the entrance on the north side, another large glacier, now named the Reid, was discovered at the head of one of the northern branches of the bay. Pushing ahead into this new fiord, we found that it was not only packed with bergs, but that the spaces between the bergs were crusted with new ice, compelling us to turn back while we were yet several miles from the discharging frontal wall. But though we were not then allowed to set foot on this magnificent glacier, we obtained a fine view of it, and I made the Indians cease rowing while I sketched its principal features. Thence, after steering northeastward a few miles, we discovered still another great glacier, now named the Carroll. But the fiord into which this glacier flows was, like the last, utterly inaccessible on account of ice, and we had to be content with a general view and a sketch of it, gained as we rowed slowly past at a distance of three or four miles. The mountains back of it and on each side of its inlet are sculptured in a singularly rich and striking style of architecture, in which subordinate peaks and gables appear in wonderful profusion, and an imposing conical mountain with a wide, smooth base stands out in the main current of the glacier, a mile or two back from the great ice-wall.

We now turned southward down the eastern shore of the bay, and in an hour or two discovered a large glacier of the second class, at the head of a comparatively short fiord that winter had not yet closed. Here we landed, and climbed across a mile or so of rough boulder-beds, and back upon the wildly broken receding snout of the glacier, which, though it descends to the level of the sea, no longer sends off bergs. Many large masses were detached from the wasting snout by irregular melting, and were buried beneath the mud, sand, gravel, and boulders of the terminal moraine. Thus protected, these fossil icebergs remain unmelted for many years, some of them for a century or more, as shown by the age of trees growing above them, though there are no trees here as yet. At length melting, a pit with sloping sides is formed by the falling of the overlying moraine material into the space at first occupied by the buried ice. In this way are formed the curious depressions in drift-covered regions called kettles, or sinks. On these decaying glaciers we may also find many interesting lessons on the formation of boulders and boulder-beds, which in all glaciated countries exert a marked influence on scenery, health, and fruitfulness.

Three or four miles farther down the bay we came to another fiord, up which we sailed in quest of more glaciers, discovering one in each of the two branches into which the fiord divides. Neither of these glaciers quite reaches tide-water. Notwithstanding their great size and the apparent fruitfulness of their fountains, they are in the first stage of decadence, the waste from melting and evaporation being greater now than the supply of new ice from the snow. We reached the one in the north branch after a comfortable scramble, and climbed over its huge, wrinkled brow, from the top of which we gained a good view of the trunk and some of the tributaries, and also of the sublime gray cliffs that tower on each hand above the ice.

Then we sailed up the south branch of the inlet, but failed to reach the glacier there, on account of a thin sheet of new ice. With the tent-poles we broke a lane for the canoe for a little distance; but it was slow, hard work, and we soon saw that we could not reach the glacier before dark. Nevertheless, we gained a fair view of it as it came sweeping down through its gigantic gateway of massive Yosemite rocks three and four thousand feet high. Here we lingered until sundown, gazing and sketching; then we turned back, and encamped on a bed of cobblestones between the forks of the fiord.

Our fire was made of fossil wood gathered on the beach. This wood is found scattered or in wave-washed windrows all about the bay where the shores are low enough for it to rest. It also occurs in abundance in many of the ravines and gorges, and in roughly stratified beds of moraine material, some of which are more than a thousand feet in thickness. The bed-rocks on which these deposits rest are scored and polished by glacial action, like all the rocks hereabouts up to at least three thousand feet above the sea. The timber is mostly in the form of broken trunks of the Merten, Paton, and Menzies spruce, the largest sections being twenty to thirty feet long, and from one to three feet in diameter, some of them, with the bark on, sound and tough. It appears, therefore, that these shores were, a century or so ago, as generously forested as those of the adjacent bays and inlets are to-day; though, strange to say, not one tree is left standing, with the exception of a few on mountain-tops near the mouth of the bay and on the east side of the Muir Glacier. How this disforestment was effected I have not space to tell here. I will only say that all I have seen goes to show that the moraine soil on which the forests were growing was held in place on the steep mountain slopes by the grand trunk glacier that recently filled the entire bay as its channel, and that when it melted the soil and forests were sloughed off together.

As we sat by the camp-fire the brightness of the sky brought on a long talk with the Indians about the stars; and their eager, childlike attention was refreshing to see as compared with the decent, deathlike apathy of weary civilized people, in whom natural curiosity has been quenched in toil and care and poor, shallow comfort.

After sleeping a few hours, I stole quietly out of the camp, and climbed the mountain that stands guard between the two glaciers. The ground was frozen, making the climbing difficult in the steepest places; but the views over the icy bay, sparkling beneath the glorious effulgence of the sky, were enchanting. It seemed then a sad thing that any part of so precious a night had been lost in sleep. The starlight was so full that I distinctly saw not only the bay with its multitude of glittering bergs, but most of the lower portions of the glaciers, lying pale and spirit-like amid the huge silent mountains. The nearest glacier in particular was so distinct that it seemed to be glowing with light that came from within itself. Not even in dark nights have I ever found any difficulty in seeing large glaciers; but on this mountain-top, amid so much ice, in the heart of so clear and frosty a night, crossed over to our Sunday storm-camp, cautiously boring a way through the bergs. We found the shore lavishly adorned with a fresh arrival of assorted bergs that had been left stranded at high tide. They were arranged in a broad, curving row, looking intensely clear and pure on the gray sand, and, with the sun-

DRAWN BY J. A. FRASER, FROM A SKETCH MADE BY THE AUTHOR IN 1879.   ENGRAVED BY C. A. POWELL.
THE HUGH MILLER GLACIER.

everything was luminous, and I seemed to be poised in a vast hollow between two skies of equal brightness. How strong I felt after my exhilarating scramble, and how glad I was that my good angel had called me before the glorious night succeeding so glorious a morning had been spent!

I got back to camp in time for an early breakfast, and by daylight we had everything packed and were again under way. The fiord was frozen nearly to its mouth, and though the ice was so thin that it gave us but little trouble in breaking a way, yet it showed us that the season for exploration in these waters was well-nigh over. We were in danger of being imprisoned in a jam of icebergs, for the water-spaces between them freeze rapidly, binding the floes into one mass. Across such floes it would be almost impossible to drag a canoe, however industriously we might ply the ax, as our Hoona guide took great pains to warn us. I would have kept straight down the bay from here, but the guide had to be taken home, and the provisions we left at the bark hut had to be got on board. We therefore beams pouring through them, suggested the jewel-paved streets of the New Jerusalem.

On our way down the coast, after examining the front of the beautiful Geikie Glacier, we obtained our first broad view of the Muir Glacier, the last of all the grand company to be seen, the stormy weather having hidden it when we first entered the bay. It was now perfectly clear, and the spacious, prairie-like glacier, with its many tributaries extending far back into the snowy recesses of the mountains, made a magnificent display of its wealth, and I was strongly tempted to go and explore it at all hazards. But winter had come, and the freezing of its fiord was an insurmountable obstacle. I had, therefore, to be content for the present with sketching and studying its main features at a distance. When we arrived at the Hoona hunting-camp, the men, women, and children came swarming out to welcome us. In the neighborhood of this camp I carefully noted the lines of demarkation between the forested and disforested regions. Several mountains here are only in part disforested, and the lines separating the bare and the forested portions are well defined. The soil, as well as the trees, had slid off the steep slopes, leaving the edges of the woods raw-looking and rugged.

At the mouth of the bay a series of moraine islands shows that the trunk glacier that occupied the bay halted here for some time, and deposited this island material as a terminal moraine; that more of the bay was not filled in shows that, after lingering here, it receded comparatively fast. All the level portions of trunks of glaciers occupying ocean fiords, instead of melting back gradually in times of general shrinking and recession, as inland glaciers with sloping channels do, melt almost uniformly over all the surface until they become thin enough to float. Then, of course, with each rise and fall of the tide the seawater, with a temperature usually considerably above the freezing-point, rushes in and out beneath them, causing rapid waste of the nether surface, while the upper is being wasted by the weather, until at length the fiord portions of these great glaciers become comparatively thin and weak, and are broken up, and vanish almost simultaneously from the mouths of their fiords to the heads of them.

Glacier Bay is undoubtedly young as yet. Vancouver's chart, made only a century ago, shows no trace of it, though found admirably faithful in general. It seems probable, therefore, that even then the entire bay was occupied by a glacier of which all those described above, great though they are, were only tributaries. Nearly as great a change has taken place in Sum Dum Bay since Vancouver's visit, the main trunk glacier there having receded from eighteen to twenty-five miles from the line marked on his chart.

The next season (1880), on September 1, I again entered Glacier Bay, and steered direct for the Muir Glacier. I was anxious to make my main camp as near the ice-wall as possible, to watch the discharge of the bergs. Toyatte, the grandest Indian I ever knew, had been killed soon after our return to Fort Wrangel; and my new captain, Tyeen, was inclined to keep at a safe distance from the "big ice-mountain," the threatening cliffs of which rose to a height of 300 feet above the water. After a good deal of urging he ventured within half a mile of them, on the east side of the fiord, where with Mr. Young I went ashore to seek a camp-ground on the moraine, leaving the Indians in the canoe. In a few minutes after we landed a huge berg sprung aloft with tremendous commotion, and the frightened Indians incontinently fled, plying their paddles in the tossing waves with admirable energy until they reached a safe shelter around the south end of the moraine, a mile down the inlet. I found a good place for a camp in a slight hollow where a few spruce stumps afforded abundance of firewood. But all efforts to get Tyeen out of his harbor failed. Nobody knew, he said, how far the ice-mountain could dash waves up the beach, and his canoe would be broken. Therefore I had my bedding and some provision carried to a high camp, and enjoyed the wildness alone.

Next morning at daybreak I pushed eagerly back over the snout and along the eastern mar-

AFTER A PHOTOGRAPH BY REID.   ENGRAVED BY C. A. POWELL.
WHITE GLACIER, A SMALL EASTERN TRIBUTARY OF THE MUIR GLACIER.

gin of the glacier, to see as much as possible of the upper fountain region. About five miles back from the front I climbed a mountain 2500 feet high, from the flowery summit of which, the day being clear, the vast glacier and all of its principal branches were displayed in one magnificent view. Instead of a stream of ice winding down a mountain-walled valley, like the largest of the Swiss glaciers, the Muir is a broad, gently undulating prairie surrounded by innumerable icy mountains, from the far, shadowy depths of which flow the many tributary glaciers that form the great central trunk. There are seven large tributaries, from two to six miles wide where they enter the trunk, and from ten to twenty miles long, each of them fed by many secondary tributaries; so that the whole number of branches, great and small, pouring from the mountain fountains must number upward of two hundred, not counting the smallest. The area drained by this one grand glacier can hardly be less than 1000 square miles, and it probably contains as much ice as all the 1100 Swiss glaciers combined. The length of the glacier from the frontal wall back to the head of the farthest fountain is estimated at fifty miles, and the width of the main trunk just below the confluence of the large tributaries is about twenty-five miles. Though apparently as motionless as the mountains, it flows on forever, the speed varying in every part with the seasons, but mostly with the depth of the current, and the declivity, smoothness, and directness of the different portions of the basin. The flow of the central cascading portion near the front, as recently determined by Professor Reid, is at the rate of from two and a half to five inches an hour, or from five to ten feet a day. A strip of the main trunk about a mile in width, extending along the eastern margin about fourteen miles to a large lake filled with bergs, has but little motion, and is so little broken by crevasses that one hundred horsemen might ride abreast over it without encountering much difficulty.

But far the greater portion of the vast expanse is torn and crumpled into a bewildering network of hummocky ridges and blades, separated by yawning gulfs and crevasses, so that the explorer, crossing the glacier from shore to shore, must always have a hard time. Here and there in the heart of the icy wilderness are spacious hollows containing beautiful lakes, fed by bands of quick-glancing streams that flow without friction in blue crystal channels, making most delightful melody, singing and ringing in silvery tones of peculiar sweetness, sun-filled crystals being the only flowers on their banks. Few, however, will be likely to enjoy them. Fortunately, to most travelers the thundering ice-wall, while comfortably accessible, is also by far the most interesting portion of the glacier.

The mountains about the great glacier were also seen from this standpoint in exceedingly grand and telling views, peaked and spired in endless variety of forms, and ranged and grouped in glorious array. Along the valleys of the main tributaries to the northwestward I saw far into their shadowy depths, one noble peak appearing beyond the other in its snowy robes in long, fading perspective. One of the most remarkable, fashioned like a superb crown with delicately fluted sides, stands in the middle of the second main tributary, counting from right to left. To the westward the majestic Fairweather Range lifted its peaks and glaciers into the blue sky in all its glory. Mount Fairweather, though not the highest, is by far the noblest of all the sky-dwelling company, the most majestic in port and architecture of all the mountains I have ever seen. It is a mountain of mountains. La Pérouse, at the south end of the range, is also a magnificent mountain, symmetrically peaked and sculptured, and wears its robes of snow and glaciers in noble style. Lituya, as seen from here, is an immense double tower, severely plain and massive. Crillon, though the loftiest of all (being nearly 16,000 feet high), presents no well-marked features. Its ponderous glaciers have ground it away into long, curling ridges until, from this point of view, it resembles a huge twisted shell. The lower summits about the Muir Glacier, like this one, the first that I climbed, are richly adorned and enlivened with beautiful flowers, though they make but a faint show in a general view. Lines and flashes of bright green appear on the lower slopes as one approaches them from the glacier, and a fainter green tinge may be noticed on the subordinate summits at a height of 2000 or 3000 feet. The lower are made mostly by alder bushes, and the topmost by a lavish profusion of flowering plants, chiefly cassiope, vaccinium, pyrola, erigeron, gentiana. campanula, anemone, larkspur, and columbine, with a few grasses and ferns. Of these cassiope is at once the commonest and the most beautiful and influential. In some places its delicate stems make mattresses on the mountain-tops two feet thick over several acres, while the bloom is so abundant that a single handful plucked at random will contain hundreds of its pale pink bells. The very thought of this, my first Alaskan glacier garden, is an exhilaration. Though it is 2500 feet high, the glacier flowed over its ground as a river flows over a boulder; and since it emerged from the icy sea as from a sepulcher it has been sorely beaten with storms; but from all those deadly, crushing, bitter experiences comes this delicate life and beauty, to teach us that what we in our faithless ignorance and fear call destruction is creation.

As I lingered here night was approaching, so I reluctantly scrambled down out of my blessed garden to the glacier, and returned to my lonely camp, and, getting some coffee and bread, again went up the moraine close to the end of the great ice-wall. The front of the glacier is about three miles wide, but the sheer middle, berg-producing portion that stretches across the inlet from side to side, like a huge green-and-blue barrier, is only about two miles wide, and its height above the water is from 250 to 300 feet. But soundings made by Captain Carroll show that 720 feet of the wall is below the surface, while a third unmeasured portion is buried beneath the moraine detritus that is constantly deposited at the foot of it. Therefore, were the water and rocky detritus cleared away, a sheer precipice of ice would be presented nearly two miles long and more than a thousand feet high. Seen from a distance, as you come up the fiord, it seems comparatively regular in form; but it is far otherwise: bold, jagged capes jut forward into the fiord, alternating with deep reëntering angles and sharp, craggy hollows with plain bastions, while the top is roughened with innumerable spires and pyramids and sharp, hacked blades leaning and toppling, or cutting straight into the sky.

The number of bergs given off varies somewhat with the weather and the tides, the average being about one every five or six minutes, counting only those large enough to thunder loudly, and make themselves heard at a distance of two or three miles. The very largest, however, may, under favorable conditions, be heard ten miles, or even farther. When a large mass sinks from the upper fissured portion of the wall, there is first a keen, piercing crash, then a deep, deliberate, prolonged, thundering roar, which slowly subsides into a low, muttering growl, followed by numerous smaller, grating, clashing sounds from the agitated bergs that dance in the waves about the newcomer as if in welcome; and these again are followed by the swash and roar of the waves that are raised and hurled against the moraines. But the largest and most beautiful of the bergs, instead of thus falling from the upper weathered portion of the wall, rise from the submerged portion with a still grander commotion, springing with tremendous voice and gestures nearly to the top of the wall, tons of water streaming like hair down their sides, plunging and rising again and again before they finally settle in perfect poise, free at last, after having formed part of a slow-crawling glacier for centuries. And as we contemplate their history, as we see them sailing past in their charming crystal beauty, how wonderful it seems that ice formed from pressed snow on the far-off mountains two or three hundred years ago should still be pure and lovely in color, after all its travel and toil in the rough mountain quarries in grinding and fashioning the face of the coming landscape! When the sunshine is sifting through the midst of this multitude of icebergs, and through the jets of radiant spray ever plashing from the blows of the falling and rising bergs, the effect is indescribably glorious. Glorious, too, are the nights along these crystal cliffs when the moon and stars are shining. Then the ice-thunder seems far louder than by day, and the projecting buttresses seem higher, as they stand forward in the pale light, relieved by the gloomy hollows, while the new bergs are dimly seen, crowned with faint lunar bows in the midst of the dashing spray. But it is in the darkest nights, when storms are blowing and the agitated waves are phosphorescent, that the most impressive displays are made. Then the long range of ice-bluffs, faintly illumined, is seen stretching through the gloom in weird, unearthly splendor, luminous foam dashing against it, and against every drifting berg; and amid all this wild, auroral splendor ever and anon some huge new-born berg dashes the living water into a yet brighter foam, and the streaming torrents pouring from its sides are worn as robes of light, while they roar in awful accord with the roaring winds, deep calling unto deep, glacier to glacier, from fiord to fiord.